Vegan Recipe Book
For a healthy life

"5 Breakfasts"

Vegan Diet:

Vegetables, fruits, nuts, seeds, legumes (beans, lentils, peas), whole grains, plant-based products such as almond milk, rice, soy, tofu, and seitan.

1. Avocado Toast with Fresh Vegetables

Ingredients:

2 slices of whole-grain bread
1 ripe avocado
Halved cherry tomatoes
Salt and pepper to taste
Freshly squeezed lemon juice
Sesame or flax seeds for garnish
Preparation:

Toast the slices of whole-grain bread until they're golden and crisp.
Slice the ripe avocado and arrange it on top of the toasted bread.
Sprinkle the halved cherry tomatoes on top, drizzle with a little fresh lemon juice.
Season with salt and pepper to taste and garnish with sesame or flax seeds for added texture and nutrition.
Serving:
Serve the avocado toast as a satisfying and healthy breakfast option.

Health Benefits:
Avocado is a great source of healthy fats, providing monounsaturated fats which may support heart health. Tomatoes contain antioxidants such as lycopene, known for its potential to reduce the risk of certain chronic diseases. Whole-grain bread offers fiber, aiding digestion and promoting a feeling of fullness.

2. Vegan Spinach and Mushroom Omelette

Ingredients:

1/2 cup crumbled tofu
1 cup fresh spinach
1/2 cup sliced mushrooms
1/4 cup chopped onion
1/2 tsp turmeric
Salt and pepper to taste
Olive oil for cooking
Preparation:

Heat a skillet over medium heat and add a little olive oil.
Sauté the onion, mushrooms, and spinach until they soften.
Add the crumbled tofu and season with turmeric, salt, and pepper. Cook for 3-4 minutes until well combined.
Serving:
Serve the vegan spinach and mushroom omelette for a protein-rich and flavorful breakfast.

Health Benefits:
Tofu is a plant-based protein, while spinach and mushrooms provide essential vitamins and minerals. Turmeric, known for its anti-inflammatory properties, is present in this recipe. Additionally, it's a low-calorie and nutrient-dense breakfast.

3. Oatmeal and Fruit Bowl

Ingredients:
- **1 cup rolled oats**
- **1 cup almond milk**
- **1 sliced banana**
- **1/2 cup fresh blueberries or strawberries**
- **1 tsp honey or maple syrup (optional)**

Preparation:
1. **Mix the rolled oats with almond milk and let them soak for 15-20 minutes.**
2. **Top with sliced banana and fresh berries.**
3. **Drizzle with honey or maple syrup if you prefer added sweetness.**

Serving: Serve this oatmeal and fruit bowl as a nutritious and filling breakfast.

Health Benefits: Oats are rich in fiber, known for supporting heart health and aiding in digestion. Fruits such as bananas and berries contribute vitamins, minerals, and antioxidants essential for overall health.

4. Vegan Pancakes with Fruit Sauce

Ingredients:

- 1 cup whole-grain flour
- 1 tsp baking powder
- 1 cup almond milk
- 2 tbsp vegetable oil
- 1 tsp sugar (optional)
- Fresh fruit sauce (blend fresh fruit of your choice)

Preparation:

1. In a bowl, combine the whole-grain flour and baking powder.
2. Gradually mix in almond milk, vegetable oil, and sugar.
3. Heat a skillet, add a ladle of the batter, and cook until bubbles form on the surface.
4. Flip the pancake and cook until golden brown.
5. Serve with fresh fruit sauce.

Health Benefits: The recipe can be made with whole-grain flour, providing more fiber and nutrients than refined flour. Fresh fruit sauce offers essential vitamins and antioxidants while replacing traditional syrup for a healthier alternative.

5. Green Smoothie Bowl

Ingredients:

1 frozen ripe banana
1 cup fresh spinach
1/2 cup almond milk
1 tbsp almond or peanut butter
Fresh fruit and seeds for topping
Preparation:

Blend the frozen banana, fresh spinach, almond milk, and almond or peanut butter until smooth.
Pour the smoothie into a bowl.
Serving:
Top the green smoothie bowl with fresh fruit and seeds for added flavor and texture.

These vegan breakfast recipes offer a variety of nutritious ingredients, easy preparation methods, and delicious serving options for a delightful morning meal. Enjoy!

Health Benefits:
This smoothie contains spinach, providing iron and other essential nutrients. It also contains healthy fats and proteins from nut butter, offering sustained energy and satiety. Including a variety of fruits and vegetables supports overall health and provides necessary vitamins and minerals.

"5 Lunches"

Vegan Diet:

Vegetables, fruits, nuts, seeds, legumes (beans, lentils, peas), whole grains, plant-based products such as almond milk, rice, soy, tofu, and seitan.

1. Quinoa Salad with Chickpeas and Veggies

Ingredients:

1 cup quinoa
1 can chickpeas, drained and rinsed
Chopped mixed vegetables (cucumber, bell pepper, cherry tomatoes)
Fresh parsley or cilantro
Olive oil and lemon juice for dressing
Salt and pepper to taste
Preparation:

Cook quinoa according to package instructions and let it cool.
In a bowl, combine quinoa, chickpeas, and chopped mixed vegetables.
Drizzle with olive oil, lemon juice, and season with salt and pepper.
Garnish with fresh herbs.
Serving:
Enjoy the quinoa salad as a refreshing and nutritious lunch option.

Health Benefits:

Quinoa provides a complete source of protein, dietary fiber, and
essential nutrients.
Chickpeas offer plant-based protein and are rich in fiber and minerals.
Mixed vegetables provide an array of vitamins, minerals, and
antioxidants for overall health.

2. Vegan Black Bean Burrito Bowl

Ingredients:

Cooked brown rice or quinoa
Canned black beans
Sliced avocado
Corn kernels
Diced red onion and bell pepper
Salsa or diced tomatoes
Lime wedges for garnish
Preparation:

Assemble the bowl with rice or quinoa as a base.
Add black beans, sliced avocado, corn, diced onion, bell pepper, and salsa.
Squeeze lime over the bowl for added flavor.
Serving:
Enjoy this burrito bowl as a flavorful and protein-packed lunch.

Health Benefits:

Brown rice or quinoa offers fiber, essential minerals, and sustained energy.
Black beans are a great source of plant-based protein, fiber, and vitamins.
Avocado provides healthy fats and various nutrients beneficial for heart health.

3. Stuffed Bell Peppers with Lentils and Rice

Ingredients:

Bell peppers (red, yellow, or green)
Cooked lentils and brown rice
Chopped onions, garlic, and tomatoes
Spices (cumin, paprika, chili powder)
Fresh parsley or cilantro for garnish
Preparation:

Preheat the oven. Cut the tops off the bell peppers and remove
seeds.
Mix cooked lentils, rice, chopped onions, garlic, tomatoes, and spices.
Stuff the peppers with the mixture and bake until peppers are tender.
Serving:
Serve the stuffed bell peppers garnished with fresh parsley or
cilantro.

Health Benefits:

Bell peppers are rich in vitamins A and C and offer antioxidants.
Lentils and brown rice provide a good source of plant-based protein
and fiber.
Garlic and onions offer antioxidants and potential health benefits for
heart health.

4. Veggie Hummus Wraps

Ingredients:

Whole-grain tortillas
Hummus
Sliced mixed vegetables (cucumbers, carrots, bell peppers)
Baby spinach or lettuce leaves
Optional: Feta cheese or avocado slices
Preparation:

Spread hummus on the tortillas.
Layer with sliced vegetables, baby spinach or lettuce, and optionally, feta cheese or avocado slices.
Roll up the tortillas and slice in half.
Serving:
Serve the veggie hummus wraps as a convenient and nutritious lunch.

Benefits:
Whole-grain tortillas provide fiber and sustained energy. Hummus offers protein, while mixed vegetables contribute vitamins and antioxidants.

5. Tofu Stir-Fry with Vegetables

Ingredients:

Cubed tofu
Sliced mixed vegetables (broccoli, bell pepper, carrots)
Soy sauce or tamari
Sesame oil
Minced garlic and ginger
Optional: Sliced green onions for garnish
Preparation:

Stir-fry tofu in a pan until golden. Set aside.
Stir-fry mixed vegetables, garlic, and ginger.
Add tofu back to the pan, drizzle with soy sauce, and cook until flavors meld.
Serving:
Serve the tofu stir-fry over brown rice or quinoa, garnished with sliced green onions.

These vegan lunch recipes offer a variety of healthy ingredients, flavorful combinations, and easy preparations for a satisfying midday meal. Enjoy!

Health Benefits:

Tofu provides plant-based protein, calcium, and is low in saturated fat.
Mixed vegetables offer an array of vitamins, minerals, and antioxidants essential for overall health.
Garlic and ginger may offer potential health benefits such as anti-inflammatory and immune-boosting properties.

"5 Dinner "

Vegan Diet:

Sure, here are five dinner recipes meeting the same requirements, including ingredients, preparation methods, serving suggestions, and health benefits

1. Vegan Lentil and Vegetable Soup

Ingredients:

1 cup lentils
Chopped mixed vegetables (carrots, celery, onions)
Vegetable broth
Garlic, thyme, and bay leaves
Olive oil
Salt and pepper to taste
Preparation:

Sauté chopped vegetables in olive oil until softened.
Add lentils, garlic, thyme, bay leaves, and vegetable broth. Simmer for
30-40 minutes.
Season with salt and pepper to taste.
Serving:
Serve the lentil and vegetable soup as a comforting and nutritious
dinner option.

2. Baked Tofu with Roasted Vegetables

Ingredients:

Tofu, cut into cubes
Assorted vegetables (bell peppers, zucchini, eggplant)
Olive oil
Herbs (rosemary, thyme)
Salt and pepper
Preparation:

Marinate tofu cubes in olive oil, herbs, salt, and pepper.
Roast tofu and mixed vegetables in the oven until golden and cooked through.
Serving:
Serve the baked tofu and roasted vegetables as a flavorful and satisfying dinner dish.

3. Vegan Stir-Fried Noodles with Tofu

Ingredients:

Tofu, sliced
Cooked noodles
Mixed vegetables (bell peppers, broccoli, carrots)
Soy sauce or teriyaki sauce
Sesame oil
Garlic and ginger
Preparation:

Sauté tofu until golden, then add mixed vegetables, garlic, and ginger.
Stir in cooked noodles, soy sauce, and sesame oil. Cook until heated through.
Serving:
Serve the stir-fried noodles and tofu as a delicious and filling dinner option.

4. Quinoa Stuffed Bell Peppers

Ingredients:

Bell peppers
Cooked quinoa
Chopped onions, tomatoes, and spinach
Italian seasoning
Olive oil
Vegan cheese (optional)
Preparation:

Cut the tops off bell peppers and remove seeds. Preheat the oven.
Mix cooked quinoa, onions, tomatoes, spinach, and seasoning.
Stuff the peppers, drizzle with olive oil, and bake until peppers are
tender.
Serving:
Serve the quinoa stuffed bell peppers, optionally topped with vegan
cheese, as a hearty and flavorful dinner.

5. Chickpea and Vegetable Curry

Ingredients:

Chickpeas
Mixed vegetables (cauliflower, peas, carrots)
Curry paste or powder
Coconut milk
Chopped cilantro for garnish
Basmati rice (optional)
Preparation:

Cook mixed vegetables in a pan, add chickpeas, curry paste, and
coconut milk. Simmer until vegetables are tender.
Garnish with chopped cilantro.
Serving:
Serve the chickpea and vegetable curry alone or with basmati rice
for a comforting and nutritious dinner option.

These dinner recipes offer a variety of wholesome ingredients,
delicious flavors, and preparation methods while providing
essential nutrients and a delightful dining experience.

"5 Breakfasts"

Vegetarian diet

These breakfast recipes provide a variety of nutrient-dense ingredients, flavors, and preparation methods, offering essential nutrients and delicious choices for a fulfilling morning meal.

1. Spinach and Feta Omelette

Ingredients:

Eggs
Chopped spinach
Crumbled feta cheese
Diced tomatoes
Olive oil
Salt and pepper
Preparation:

Whisk eggs in a bowl.
Sauté spinach and tomatoes in olive oil in a pan until wilted.
Pour the whisked eggs into the pan, sprinkle with feta cheese, salt, and pepper. Cook until set.
Serving:
Serve the spinach and feta omelette folded over with a side of whole-grain toast for a nutritious breakfast.

Benefits:
Eggs provide quality protein and essential nutrients, while spinach offers vitamins and minerals. Feta cheese contributes calcium and protein.

2. Greek Yogurt Parfait

Ingredients:

Greek yogurt
Granola
Mixed fresh berries (strawberries, blueberries, raspberries)
Honey or maple syrup (optional)
Chopped nuts (optional)
Preparation:

Layer Greek yogurt, granola, and mixed berries in a bowl or glass.
Optionally, drizzle honey or maple syrup and sprinkle chopped nuts.
Serving:
Serve the Greek yogurt parfait as a light and protein-packed breakfast option.

Benefits:
Greek yogurt offers probiotics and protein. Berries provide antioxidants and fiber, while granola and nuts offer healthy fats and additional nutrients.

3. Avocado Toast with Poached Egg

Ingredients:

Whole-grain bread
Ripe avocado
Poached egg
Lemon juice
Red pepper flakes (optional)
Salt and pepper
Preparation:

Mash ripe avocado with lemon juice, red pepper flakes, salt, and pepper.
Toast whole-grain bread and spread the mashed avocado on top.
Top with a poached egg.
Serving:
Serve the avocado toast with a poached egg for a satisfying and nutrient-rich breakfast.

Benefits:
Avocado provides healthy fats and essential nutrients. Poached eggs offer protein, vitamins, and minerals.

4. Vegetable and Cheese Frittata

Ingredients:

Eggs
Chopped mixed vegetables (bell peppers, onions, zucchini)
Grated cheese (cheddar, mozzarella)
Olive oil
Herbs (parsley, thyme)
Preparation:

Whisk eggs and mix with chopped vegetables, cheese, and herbs.
Heat olive oil in an oven-safe pan, pour in the egg mixture, and cook until edges are set.
Transfer to the oven and bake until the frittata is cooked through.
Serving:
Serve the vegetable and cheese frittata cut into wedges for a fulfilling breakfast.

Benefits:
Eggs provide protein and essential nutrients, while mixed vegetables offer vitamins and antioxidants.

5. Peanut Butter and Banana Smoothie

Ingredients:

Ripe bananas
Peanut butter
Almond milk
Chia seeds
Honey (optional)
Preparation:

Blend ripe bananas, peanut butter, almond milk, and chia seeds until smooth.
Optionally, sweeten with honey.
Serving:
Serve the peanut butter and banana smoothie as a quick and nutritious breakfast option.

Benefits:
Bananas offer potassium and fiber. Peanut butter provides protein and healthy fats, while chia seeds add omega-3 fatty acids and fiber.

"5 Lunch"

Vegetarian diet

These lunch recipes offer a variety of nutrient-rich ingredients, flavors, and preparation methods, providing essential nutrients and delicious choices for a satisfying midday meal.

1. Quinoa and Roasted Vegetable Salad

Ingredients:

Quinoa
Assorted roasted vegetables (bell peppers, zucchini, cherry
tomatoes)
Mixed greens (spinach, arugula)
Olive oil and balsamic vinegar
Feta cheese (optional)
Salt and pepper
Preparation:

Cook quinoa according to package instructions and let it cool.
Roast assorted vegetables in the oven until tender and slightly
charred.
Toss quinoa and roasted vegetables with mixed greens, drizzle
with olive oil, balsamic vinegar, and season with salt and pepper.
Optionally, top with crumbled feta cheese.
Serving:
Serve the quinoa and roasted vegetable salad as a nutritious and
hearty lunch option.

Benefits:
Quinoa is a complete protein and a great source of fiber.
Roasted vegetables offer vitamins and antioxidants, while mixed
greens add additional nutrients.

2. Caprese Pasta Salad

Ingredients:

Cooked pasta
Fresh mozzarella balls
Cherry tomatoes
Fresh basil leaves
Olive oil and balsamic glaze
Salt and pepper
Preparation:

Cook pasta according to package instructions and let it cool.
Mix pasta, fresh mozzarella balls, cherry tomatoes, and torn
basil leaves.
Drizzle with olive oil, balsamic glaze, and season with salt and
pepper.
Serving:
Serve the Caprese pasta salad as a refreshing and light lunch.

Benefits:
Pasta offers sustained energy from complex carbohydrates.
Fresh mozzarella provides calcium and protein, while tomatoes
and basil contribute vitamins and antioxidants.

3. Lentil and Vegetable Stir-Fry

Ingredients:

Cooked lentils
Mixed stir-fry vegetables (bell peppers, broccoli, snap peas)
Soy sauce or teriyaki sauce
Olive oil
Garlic and ginger
Preparation:

Sauté mixed vegetables, garlic, and ginger in olive oil until crisp-
tender.
Add cooked lentils and stir in the sauce. Cook until heated through.
Serving:
Serve the lentil and vegetable stir-fry for a quick and protein-rich
lunch.

Benefits:
Lentils are high in protein and fiber. Mixed stir-fry vegetables offer
vitamins and minerals essential for overall health.

4. Veggie Hummus Wraps

Ingredients:

Whole-grain tortillas
Hummus
Sliced mixed vegetables (cucumbers, carrots, bell peppers)
Baby spinach or lettuce leaves
Optional: Feta cheese or avocado slices
Preparation:

Spread hummus on the tortillas.
Layer with sliced vegetables, baby spinach or lettuce, and
optionally, feta cheese or avocado slices.
Roll up the tortillas and slice in half.
Serving:
Serve the veggie hummus wraps as a convenient and nutritious
lunch.

Benefits:
Whole-grain tortillas provide fiber and sustained energy. Hummus
offers protein, while mixed vegetables contribute vitamins and
antioxidants.

5. Eggplant Parmesan

Ingredients:

Sliced eggplant
Breadcrumbs
Marinara sauce
Mozzarella cheese
Grated Parmesan cheese
Olive oil
Fresh basil for garnish
Preparation:

Dip eggplant slices in breadcrumbs and bake until golden and crispy.
Layer baked eggplant with marinara sauce, mozzarella, and Parmesan cheese. Bake until cheese melts.
Garnish with fresh basil.
Serving:
Serve the eggplant parmesan with a side salad for a filling and flavorful lunch.

Benefits:
Eggplant is rich in fiber and antioxidants. Mozzarella and Parmesan provide protein and calcium, while fresh basil adds additional nutrients.

"5 Dinner"

Vegetarian diet

These dinner recipes offer
a variety of nutrient-dense
ingredients, flavorful
combinations, and
preparation methods,
contributing to essential
nutrients and a delightful
dining experience.

1. Vegetarian Chickpea Curry

Ingredients:

Chickpeas
Diced mixed vegetables (such as bell peppers, cauliflower, peas)
Curry paste or powder
Coconut milk
Chopped cilantro for garnish
Basmati rice (optional)
Preparation:

Sauté mixed vegetables in a pan and add chickpeas, curry paste,
and coconut milk. Simmer until vegetables are tender.
Garnish with chopped cilantro.
Serving:
Serve the vegetarian chickpea curry alone or with basmati rice for a
comforting and nutritious dinner option.

Benefits:
Chickpeas are an excellent source of protein and fiber. Mixed
vegetables offer vitamins and antioxidants, while coconut milk
provides healthy fats.

2. Vegetable Stir-Fry with Tofu

Ingredients:

Cubed tofu
Sliced mixed vegetables (broccoli, bell peppers, carrots)
Soy sauce or teriyaki sauce
Sesame oil
Minced garlic and ginger
Preparation:

Stir-fry tofu until golden, then add mixed vegetables, garlic, and ginger.
Stir in soy sauce and sesame oil. Cook until the flavors meld.
Serving:
Serve the vegetable stir-fry with tofu over brown rice or quinoa for a delicious and filling dinner.

Benefits:
Tofu provides protein and essential nutrients, while mixed vegetables offer vitamins and antioxidants.

3. Stuffed Bell Peppers with Quinoa and Black Beans

Ingredients:

Bell peppers
Cooked quinoa
Black beans
Chopped onions, tomatoes, and cilantro
Mexican seasoning blend
Shredded cheese (optional)
Preparation:

Preheat the oven. Cut the tops off bell peppers and remove seeds.
Mix cooked quinoa, black beans, onions, tomatoes, cilantro, and
seasoning.
Stuff the peppers and bake until they're tender.
Serving:
Serve the stuffed bell peppers, optionally topped with shredded
cheese, as a hearty and flavorful dinner.

Benefits:
Quinoa is a complete protein and a source of fiber. Black beans
offer protein and essential minerals.

4. Eggplant and Zucchini Parmesan

Ingredients:

**Sliced eggplant and zucchini
Breadcrumbs
Marinara sauce
Mozzarella cheese
Grated Parmesan cheese
Olive oil
Fresh basil for garnish
Preparation:**

**Dip eggplant and zucchini slices in breadcrumbs and bake until golden and crispy.
Layer baked slices with marinara sauce, mozzarella, and Parmesan cheese. Bake until cheese melts.
Garnish with fresh basil.
Serving:
Serve the eggplant and zucchini parmesan with a side salad for a satisfying dinner.**

**Benefits:
Eggplant and zucchini are rich in fiber and antioxidants. Mozzarella and Parmesan offer protein and calcium.**

5. Mushroom and Spinach Lasagna

Ingredients:

Lasagna noodles
Sliced mushrooms
Chopped spinach
Ricotta cheese
Marinara sauce
Shredded mozzarella cheese
Olive oil
Preparation:

Sauté mushrooms and spinach in olive oil until softened.
Layer lasagna noodles with sautéed vegetables, ricotta cheese,
marinara sauce, and mozzarella. Repeat layers.
Bake until the lasagna is cooked through.
Serving:
Serve the mushroom and spinach lasagna with a side of garlic
bread for a flavorful and satisfying dinner.

Benefits:
Mushrooms and spinach offer essential vitamins and minerals.
Ricotta and mozzarella cheeses provide protein and calcium.

"5 Breakfasts"

The gluten-free diet

These breakfast recipes offer a variety of gluten-free options rich in nutrients, flavors, and easy preparation methods, providing essential nutrients and delicious choices for a satisfying morning meal.

1. Quinoa Breakfast Bowl

Ingredients:

Cooked quinoa
Sliced fresh fruits (strawberries, bananas, blueberries)
Chopped nuts (almonds, walnuts)
Honey or maple syrup (optional)
Cinnamon for garnish
Preparation:

Arrange a bowl with cooked quinoa.
Top with sliced fresh fruits and chopped nuts.
Optionally, drizzle with honey or maple syrup and sprinkle with cinnamon.
Serving:
Serve the quinoa breakfast bowl as a wholesome and nutrient-rich morning meal.

Benefits:
Quinoa offers protein and essential nutrients. Fresh fruits provide vitamins and antioxidants, while nuts offer healthy fats and additional nutrients.

2. Veggie Omelette with Spinach and Bell Peppers

Ingredients:

Eggs
Chopped spinach
Diced bell peppers
Olive oil
Salt and pepper
Preparation:

Whisk eggs in a bowl.
Sauté chopped spinach and diced bell peppers in a pan until wilted.
Pour the whisked eggs into the pan, season with salt and pepper. Cook until set.
Serving:
Serve the veggie omelette as a protein-rich and fulfilling breakfast option.

Benefits:
Eggs offer high-quality protein and essential nutrients.
Spinach and bell peppers provide vitamins and antioxidants.

3. Almond Flour Pancakes

Ingredients:

Almond flour
Eggs
Almond milk
Baking powder
Vanilla extract
Maple syrup for topping
Preparation:

Mix almond flour, eggs, almond milk, baking powder, and vanilla
extract in a bowl to form a batter.
Cook pancakes on a skillet until golden brown.
Serving:
Serve the almond flour pancakes with maple syrup for a delightful
gluten-free breakfast.

Benefits:
Almond flour offers a gluten-free alternative with added protein
and healthy fats. Eggs contribute protein and essential nutrients.

4. Greek Yogurt Parfait with Granola

Ingredients:

Greek yogurt
Gluten-free granola
Mixed fresh berries (strawberries, raspberries)
Honey or agave syrup (optional)
Preparation:

Layer Greek yogurt and gluten-free granola in a glass or bowl.
Top with mixed fresh berries.
Optionally, drizzle with honey or agave syrup.
Serving:
Serve the Greek yogurt parfait as a refreshing and protein-rich breakfast option.

Benefits:
Greek yogurt provides probiotics and protein. Berries offer antioxidants and fiber, while gluten-free granola adds sustained energy.

5. Avocado and Smoked Salmon Toast

Ingredients:

Sliced gluten-free bread
Ripe avocado
Smoked salmon
Lemon juice
Fresh dill for garnish
Salt and pepper
Preparation:

Toast gluten-free bread slices until crispy.
Mash ripe avocado with lemon juice, salt, and pepper. Spread on
the toast.
Top with slices of smoked salmon and garnish with fresh dill.
Serving:
Serve the avocado and smoked salmon toast for a nutrient-rich and
satisfying breakfast.

Benefits:
Avocado provides healthy fats and essential nutrients. Smoked
salmon offers high-quality protein and omega-3 fatty acids.

"5 Lunches"

The gluten-free diet

These lunch recipes offer a diverse selection of gluten-free ingredients, flavors, and simple preparation methods, contributing to essential nutrients and a delightful dining experience.

1. Quinoa Salad with Grilled Chicken

Ingredients:

Cooked quinoa
Grilled chicken breast strips
Chopped mixed vegetables (cucumber, cherry tomatoes, bell peppers)
Olive oil and lemon juice for dressing
Salt and pepper to taste
Fresh herbs for garnish

Preparation:

Mix cooked quinoa, grilled chicken strips, and chopped mixed vegetables in a bowl.
Drizzle with olive oil, lemon juice, and season with salt and pepper.
Garnish with fresh herbs.

Serving:

Serve the quinoa salad with grilled chicken as a protein-rich and satisfying lunch option.

Benefits:

Quinoa offers protein and essential nutrients. Grilled chicken provides lean protein, while mixed vegetables offer vitamins and antioxidants.

2. Lentil Soup with Mixed Vegetables

Ingredients:

Cooked lentils
Diced mixed vegetables (carrots, celery, onions)
Gluten-free vegetable broth
Olive oil
Garlic, thyme, and bay leaves
Salt and pepper
Preparation:

Sauté diced mixed vegetables in olive oil until softened.
Add cooked lentils, garlic, thyme, bay leaves, and vegetable broth.
Simmer for 30-40 minutes.
Season with salt and pepper.
Serving:
Serve the lentil soup with mixed vegetables as a comforting and
nutrient-rich lunch.

Benefits:
Lentils offer protein and fiber. Mixed vegetables provide vitamins
and antioxidants, supporting overall health.

3. Quinoa Stuffed Bell Peppers

Ingredients:

Bell peppers
Cooked quinoa
Chopped onions, tomatoes, and spinach
Italian seasoning
Olive oil
Shredded cheese (optional)
Preparation:

Preheat the oven. Cut the tops off bell peppers and remove seeds.
Mix cooked quinoa, onions, tomatoes, spinach, and seasoning.
Stuff the peppers, drizzle with olive oil, and bake until they're tender.
Serving:
Serve the quinoa stuffed bell peppers, optionally topped with shredded cheese, as a hearty and flavorful lunch.

Benefits:
Quinoa offers protein and essential nutrients. Mixed vegetables provide vitamins and antioxidants.

4. Rice Paper Spring Rolls with Shrimp and Vegetables

Ingredients:

Rice paper wrappers
Cooked shrimp
Sliced mixed vegetables (cabbage, carrots, cucumber)
Fresh herbs (mint, cilantro)
Gluten-free hoisin or peanut sauce
Preparation:

Soak rice paper wrappers in warm water until pliable.
Layer cooked shrimp and sliced mixed vegetables on the wrappers.
Add fresh herbs and roll tightly. Serve with dipping sauce.
Serving:
Serve the rice paper spring rolls with shrimp and vegetables as a
light and refreshing lunch.

Benefits:
Shrimp offers protein and essential nutrients. Mixed vegetables
provide vitamins and antioxidants, while rice paper offers a gluten-
free alternative.

5. Quinoa and Black Bean Wraps

Ingredients:

Cooked quinoa
Black beans
Sliced mixed vegetables (bell peppers, onions)
Gluten-free tortillas
Olive oil
Taco seasoning (gluten-free)
Optional: Avocado slices, salsa
Preparation:

Sauté sliced mixed vegetables in olive oil until tender.
Mix cooked quinoa, black beans, and taco seasoning.
Fill tortillas with the quinoa and black bean mixture, sautéed vegetables, and optional toppings.
Serving:
Serve the quinoa and black bean wraps for a flavorful and protein-rich lunch.

Benefits:
Quinoa offers protein and essential nutrients. Black beans provide protein and fiber, while mixed vegetables contribute vitamins and antioxidants.

"5 Dinner"

The gluten-free diet

These dinner recipes offer a variety of gluten-free ingredients, flavors, and preparation methods, providing essential nutrients and delicious choices for a fulfilling evening meal.

1. Baked Salmon with Quinoa and Roasted Vegetables

Ingredients:

Salmon fillets
Cooked quinoa
Assorted roasted vegetables (bell peppers, zucchini, cherry
tomatoes)
Olive oil
Lemon wedges for garnish
Salt and pepper
Preparation:

Preheat the oven. Arrange salmon fillets on a baking sheet and
season with salt and pepper.
Bake the salmon until cooked through.
Serve with a side of cooked quinoa and roasted vegetables tossed in
olive oil.
Serving:
Serve the baked salmon with quinoa and roasted vegetables as a
nutrient-rich and fulfilling dinner.

Benefits:
Salmon provides omega-3 fatty acids and protein. Quinoa offers
protein and essential nutrients, while roasted vegetables supply
vitamins and antioxidants.

2. Stir-Fried Tofu with Gluten-Free Teriyaki Sauce

Ingredients:

Tofu, cubed
Sliced mixed vegetables (bell peppers, broccoli, carrots)
Gluten-free teriyaki sauce
Olive oil
Minced garlic and ginger
Preparation:

Sauté tofu cubes in olive oil until golden.
Add sliced mixed vegetables, garlic, and ginger. Stir-fry until vegetables are crisp-tender.
Stir in gluten-free teriyaki sauce and cook until heated through.
Serving:
Serve the stir-fried tofu and mixed vegetables for a flavorful and satisfying dinner.

Benefits:
Tofu provides protein and essential nutrients. Mixed vegetables offer vitamins and antioxidants, and the teriyaki sauce adds flavor without gluten.

3. Grilled Chicken with Quinoa Salad

Ingredients:

Grilled chicken breast
Cooked quinoa
Diced mixed vegetables (cucumber, cherry tomatoes, bell peppers)
Olive oil and lemon juice for dressing
Salt and pepper
Fresh herbs for garnish
Preparation:

Mix cooked quinoa and diced mixed vegetables in a bowl.
Season the quinoa salad with olive oil, lemon juice, salt, and pepper.
Serve with grilled chicken breast and garnish with fresh herbs.
Serving:
Serve the grilled chicken with quinoa salad as a protein-rich and
nutritious dinner option.

Benefits:
Grilled chicken provides lean protein. Quinoa offers protein and
essential nutrients, while mixed vegetables supply vitamins and
antioxidants.

4. Gluten-Free Pasta with Pesto and Shrimp

Ingredients:

Gluten-free pasta
Shrimp
Homemade or store-bought pesto sauce (gluten-free)
Olive oil
Garlic and red pepper flakes (optional)
Parmesan cheese (optional)
Preparation:

Cook the gluten-free pasta according to package instructions.
Sauté shrimp in olive oil and garlic until pink.
Toss cooked pasta with pesto sauce and cooked shrimp. Optionally, add red pepper flakes and Parmesan cheese.
Serving:
Serve the gluten-free pasta with pesto and shrimp as a flavorful and filling dinner.

Benefits:
Shrimp provides protein and essential nutrients. Gluten-free pasta offers an alternative for those with gluten sensitivities, while pesto adds flavor without gluten.

5. Baked Quinoa and Black Bean Stuffed Bell Peppers

Ingredients:

Bell peppers
Cooked quinoa
Black beans
Diced tomatoes, onions, and cilantro
Mexican seasoning blend
Olive oil
Preparation:

Preheat the oven. Cut the tops off bell peppers and remove seeds.
Mix cooked quinoa, black beans, diced tomatoes, onions, cilantro, and seasoning.
Stuff the peppers, drizzle with olive oil, and bake until tender.
Serving:
Serve the baked quinoa and black bean stuffed bell peppers as a flavorful and wholesome dinner.

Benefits:
Quinoa provides protein and essential nutrients. Black beans offer protein and fiber, while mixed vegetables contribute vitamins and antioxidants.

"5 Dessert"

Vegan Dessert

These dinner dessert recipes offer a selection of healthy, flavorful options, adhering to dietary preferences and providing essential nutrients while satisfying those sweet cravings.

1. Chia Seed Pudding

Ingredients:

Chia seeds
Unsweetened almond milk (or any preferred milk)
Vanilla extract
Fresh fruit for topping (e.g., berries, sliced bananas)
Optional: Honey or maple syrup for sweetening
Preparation:

Mix chia seeds, almond milk, and vanilla extract in a bowl or jar.
Stir well and refrigerate for a few hours or overnight until it
thickens.
Serve topped with fresh fruit and a drizzle of honey or maple syrup
if desired.
Benefits:
Chia seeds offer omega-3 fatty acids and fiber. Almond milk is a
dairy-free alternative rich in vitamins and minerals.

2. Baked Apple Slices with Cinnamon

Ingredients:

Sliced apples
Cinnamon powder
Optional: Stevia or honey for sweetness
Preparation:

Preheat the oven. Place apple slices on a baking sheet.
Sprinkle with cinnamon and a natural sweetener if desired.
Bake until tender and lightly caramelized.
Serving:
Serve warm baked apple slices as a guilt-free and comforting dessert.

Benefits:
Apples are a good source of fiber and various vitamins. Cinnamon offers antioxidants and potential health benefits.

3. Dark Chocolate Avocado Mousse

Ingredients:

Ripe avocados
Dark chocolate (70% or higher)
Cocoa powder
Maple syrup or agave nectar for sweetness
Preparation:

Blend ripe avocados, melted dark chocolate, cocoa powder, and sweetener until smooth.
Chill in the refrigerator for a few hours.
Serving:
Serve the dark chocolate avocado mousse chilled as a rich and creamy dessert option.

Benefits:
Avocados provide healthy fats and essential nutrients. Dark chocolate offers antioxidants and potential health benefits in moderation.

4. Coconut Milk Rice Pudding

Ingredients:

Cooked white or brown rice
Coconut milk
Coconut sugar or alternative sweetener
Shredded coconut for garnish
Optional: Cinnamon or nutmeg for flavor
Preparation:

In a pot, combine cooked rice, coconut milk, and
sweetener.
Simmer until the mixture thickens. Add more milk if
needed.
Garnish with shredded coconut and spices if desired.
Serving:
Serve the coconut milk rice pudding warm or chilled for a
delightful dessert.

Benefits:
Coconut milk offers healthy fats, while rice provides
sustenance and energy.

5. Berry Sorbet

Ingredients:

Mixed frozen berries
Fresh lemon juice
Agave syrup or sweetener (optional)
Preparation:

Blend frozen berries, lemon juice, and sweetener until smooth.
Transfer to a container and freeze until firm.
Serving:
Serve the berry sorbet as a refreshing and naturally sweet dessert.

Benefits:
Berries are rich in antioxidants and various vitamins, promoting overall health and well-being. Lemon offers a zesty tang and vitamin C.

Notes

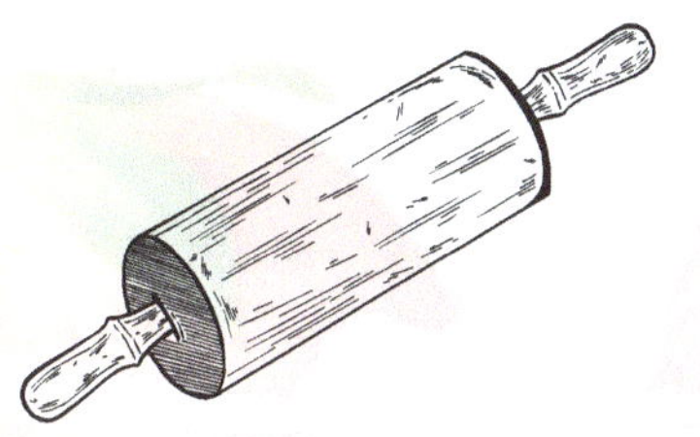

Notes

Notes

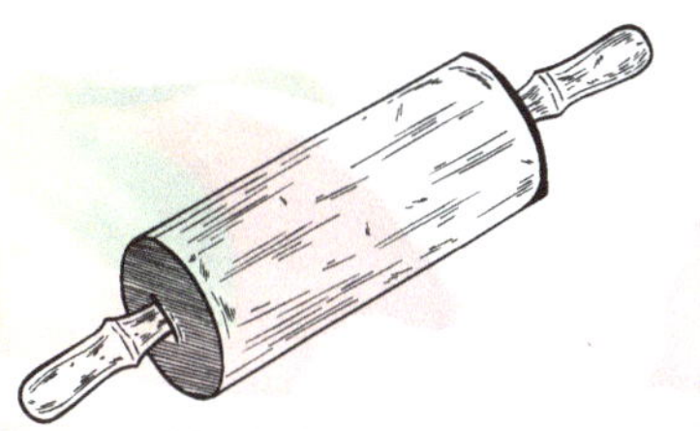

Notes

Notes

Notes

Notes

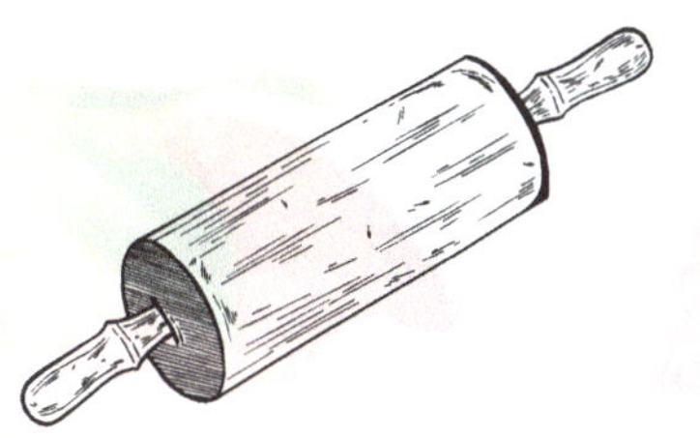

Notes

Notes

Notes

Notes

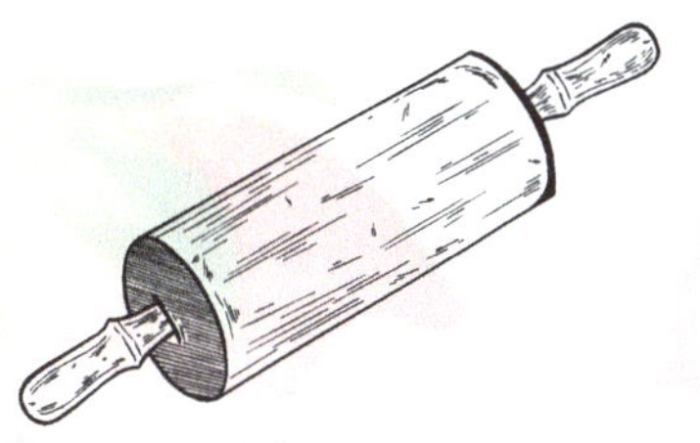

Notes

Notes

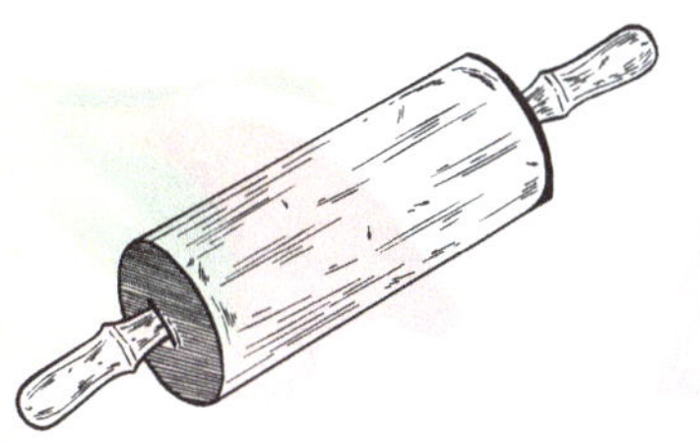 

Notes

Notes

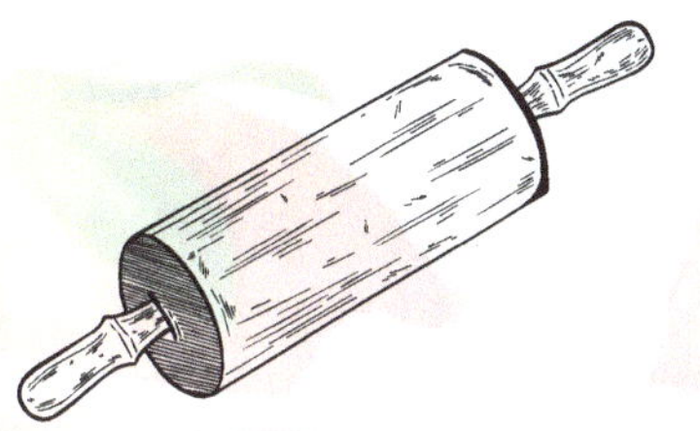

Notes

Hi there! This is Tande,a father,graphic designer and children's book author from Europe.Book reviews are incredibly important when it comes to making book sales.If you wouldn't mind taking one minute out of your day toreview this coloring book it would be greatly appreciated i read every review and take all feedback into consideration when designing and creating new books .Thank you!
Sincerty